PRAYING 101
for
SPIRITUAL ENLIGHTENMENT

By

Dottie Randazzo

Praying 101
for
Spiritual Enlightenment

by
Dottie Randazzo

Creative Dreaming
6433 Topanga Cyn. Blvd.
120
Woodland Hills, CA 91303

All rights reserved. No part of this book may be reproduced or transmitted in any form or by any means, electronic or mechanical, including photocopying, recording or by any information storage and retrieval system, without permission from the author, except for the inclusion of brief quotations in a review.

Copyright © 2007 by Dottie Randazzo

ISBN 978-0-6151-4010-0

The most powerful form of energy one can generate is not mechanical, electronic or even atomic energy, but prayer energy.

Alexis Carrel

By Dottie Randazzo

Praying 101 for Spiritual Enlightenment
Praying 101 for Kids & Teens
Praying 101 for Men
Praying 101 for Women
Praying 101 for Parents

Introduction

I realized a long time ago that most people think that their prayers are not heard because they are not getting what they want. It's not that their prayer wasn't heard; it's all in the asking. A few years ago someone told me that they wanted something and I asked if they had said a prayer for it. They told me that they didn't know how to pray.

As a child I was never taught how to pray. I attended both Baptist and Lutheran schools where I was taught how to memorize a few really good prayers, such as the Lord's Prayer.

I know how to pray. I am not sure how I learned, but I did. All you have to do is ask my sister and she will tell you. She has often said I have a direct line to the heavens.

This book will teach you how to pray. It is your basic prayer book. I have designed a prayer for many aspects of your life. Once you have learned the key ingredients to praying you will have the tools to customize your own prayers. So let's flip the page and begin to solve the mystery of prayer.

Commonly Asked Questions

Do I need to know any special language to pray?

You do not need to know any special language. Your language and words will be understood.

Who do I pray to?

It does not matter whether you are praying to God. Our Father, The Masters of the Universe, or whomever, your prayer will be heard. Pray to the One that you believe in.

When and where should I pray?

Praying can be done anytime and anywhere. If you want to say your prayer in the morning, then that is when you should say it. If you want to say your prayer while talking a walk, then that's when you should.

Do I have to kneel down or say my prayer out loud?

No kneeling needed. You can sit, lie down or be sitting in a park. It doesn't matter; your prayer will be heard. Your prayer does not need to be said out loud.

How do I pray?

To pray you use the little voice in your head. The same one that you hear when someone walks into the room with a weird hairdo and you hear in your head, *what was she thinking with that hair?* That's the same voice that you are going to say your prayer with. Those same voices in your head that you hear say, *I did well* or *I should not have done that*. It is almost like talking to yourself except you do it in your head. Say your prayer just like you are writing a letter; begin with "Dear____." And always end your prayer with thanks. Thanks for listening, thanks for caring, thanks for looking out for me. Gratitude goes a long way in life.

If I don't get what I am asking for, does that mean my prayer was not heard?

Not getting what you want absolutely does not mean that your prayer was not heard. We always get what we want. We may not get it when we want it. We get it when we are supposed to.

We should not be discouraged if our prayers go unanswered; if some were, we most certainly would have grave reservations about the sanity of God.

J.K. Stuart

Very Important Things You Should Know

Everything happens for a reason. If something bad happens to you, you need to look at the experience and see what you were supposed to learn from it. For example, the yoga class that you show up for is full. You feel disappointed. You attend the next yoga class that is available and meet a new friend. Had you been able to get into your regular yoga class you would have never met this person.

Everything happens exactly when it is supposed to. This might not be when you want it to happen. For example, you decide to begin a project. You get a million interruptions and don't seem to be getting anywhere with your project. You get discouraged and put it away. Sometime later, maybe days, months or even years you pick it up and breeze right through the project with little or no interruptions at all. You should always know what you want to accomplish in life. The Universe will provide the way when the time is right.

You are doing in your life exactly what you are supposed to be doing at this exact moment. Every single moment in your life is very important and every single moment in your life affects the next moment in your life. Every person that you meet has a reason to be in your life, even if just for a brief moment. Some people come into our lives for a reason and some for a season.

Enjoy your life. You must learn to enjoy your life. Eating your breakfast in the morning is part of your life. Don't sit down and eat it fast while you are thinking of something else. This is a very bad habit to start. It will take you twice as long to fix the bad habit. Every single day is a very important day in your life. It is a day that you will never get to relive. Learn to appreciate every moment and don't take them for granted.

Pray for wisdom. Wisdom is smarts, answers, solutions and brainpower. When you ask for wisdom you ask to be aware of the right answers. Wisdom allows you to see answers when they enter your life. For example, have you ever wondered about something and then suddenly you get a phone call, pick up a book or talk to someone who can provide the answer about that thing that you were wondering about? It happens all the time. If you take time to reflect you will see it happens more than you imagined. Remember the Universe always sends us what we need, when we need it. Sometimes we get answers but they do not always come to us the way we think that they should and therefore we don't see the answer. We miss them because we are looking for them to be delivered our way. Answers are delivered the way that they are supposed to be delivered, not necessarily the way that we want them delivered.

Believe that your prayers are heard and will be answered. Why pray if you don't have any faith. The bible says that faith the size of a mustard seed can move a mountain. Like Wow! Have you ever seen a mustard seed? It's tiny. Don't try praying to test the system. It doesn't work. The system does not need to be tested by you.

Prayer for Self-Reliance

Dear Lord,

I pray for the wisdom to be my own best friend. I pray for the wisdom to provide for myself emotionally and physically. I pray for the wisdom, strength and courage to filter out negativity that may sway me from listening to my inner voice. I pray for the wisdom, strength and courage to not let others talk me out of fulfilling my dreams. I pray for the wisdom to recognize that I am as qualified and deserving of achievement as any other person is. I pray for the wisdom to turn to my inner source for direction. Thank you for caring about me.

Prayer for Detoxification

Dear God,

I pray for the wisdom, strength and courage to release the toxins from my mind, body and heart. I pray for the wisdom, strength and courage to release my cravings of harmful habits. I pray for the wisdom to take excellent care of my body. Thank you for blessing me.

Prayer for Inner Power

Dear Masters of the Universe,

I pray for the wisdom to allow myself to experience and express my true power. I pray for the wisdom to recognize opportunities to expand my power in ways that bring great blessings to me and the world. I pray for the wisdom, strength and courage to release any fears I have about being powerful. I pray for the wisdom to keep my self-esteem high by honoring myself, taking care of my physical and emotional self, working on my dreams and aspirations by spending time in prayer and meditation. Thank you for taking care of me.

Prayer for Miracle Healing

Dear Goddess,

I pray for assistance in my healing. I pray for the wisdom, strength and courage to completely surrender my situation to you. Thank you for listening to me.

Prayer to Break Free

Dear Higher Power,

I pray for the wisdom to free myself from any unnatural restrictions. I pray for the strength and courage to not be controlled by my addictions. I pray for assistance in releasing my fears and breaking free. I pray for the strength and courage to be responsible. Thank you for listening to me.

Prayer to Trust Your Intuition

Dear Father,

I pray for the wisdom, strength and courage to follow my heart's path. I pray for the knowledge of what to do. I pray for the wisdom, strength and courage to trust and follow my inner voice. I pray for the wisdom to not ignore messages or procrastinate. I pray for the wisdom, strength and courage to trust and follow my feelings and thoughts without question or delay. Thank you for taking care of me.

Prayer to Surrender

Dear Lord,

I pray for the wisdom, strength and courage to surrender any attachment to my appearance. I pray for the wisdom, strength and courage to surrender feelings of shame, fear, anger, resentment and control. I pray for the wisdom to recognize that the Universe always works for my good. Thank you for blessing me.

Prayer to be Good to Yourself

Dear God,

I pray for the wisdom to understand that any confusion or changes I am currently experiencing are part of my healthy evolution. I pray for the wisdom to follow my intuition. I pray for the wisdom to build a solid foundation of truth. I pray for the strength and courage to admit my true feelings to myself. I pray for the wisdom to get in touch with my deepest feelings. I pray for the strength and courage to be honest with myself and others. I pray for the wisdom to listen and follow my true feelings. Thank you for listening to me.

Prayer to Remove Guilt

Dear Masters of the Universe,

I pray for the wisdom, strength and courage to always be free to choose. I pray for the wisdom that my choices will always be in alignment with the Universe. If my choices are not the correct ones, I pray for the wisdom to make another choice. I pray to have the guilt removed if I make the wrong choice. Thank you for taking care of me.

Prayer for Financial Success

Dear Goddess,

I pray for any financial blocks to be removed. I pray for the wisdom to have continued positive thoughts. I pray for the wisdom to identify any guilt or negative feelings that I have regarding money. Thank you for blessing me.

Prayer for Kindness

Dear Higher Power,

I pray for the wisdom, strength and courage to practice kindness in all of my thoughts and deeds today. I pray for the wisdom to recognize the rewards that come my way. I pray for the wisdom to practice kindness towards animals, people, plants and the planet. Thank you for listening to me.

Prayer for Feeling Safe

Dear Father,

I pray that you remove any feelings of vulnerability I may feel. I pray for protection. I pray for the wisdom and power to create a happy and secure life. Thank you for blessing me.

Prayer for Trust

Dear God,

I pray for the wisdom, strength and courage to put my trust in the Universe. I pray for the wisdom to be guided and protected. I pray for the courage to trust that everything that affects me will be handled by the Universe. I pray for the courage to trust that unpleasant events that occur in my life occur for me to learn from. Thank you for taking care of me.

Prayer for Family Harmony

Dear Lord,

I pray for the wisdom to hold loving thoughts and feelings about my friends and family (including myself). I pray for the wisdom to send loving energy to each person I come in contact with. I pray for patience in the healing of family relationships. I give thanks for each person in my family. I pray for the wisdom, strength and courage to love the individuals who frustrate me. I pray for the wisdom to see the goodness in everyone I meet. Thank you for blessing me.

Prayer for Resolution

Dear Masters of the Universe,

I pray for the wisdom, strength and courage to let go of the problem I have been struggling to resolve. I pray for the wisdom, strength and courage to surrender this situation to the Universe. I pray for the courage to trust in the power of the Universe. Thank you for taking care of me.

Prayer for Discipline

Dear Higher Power,

I pray for the wisdom, strength and courage to love myself enough to take care of myself. I pray for the wisdom, strength and courage to attend to my life in a disciplined way. I pray for the wisdom to see the areas in my life in which I need to employ more discipline. Thank you for listening to me.

Prayer for Higher Consciousness

Dear Father,

I pray for guidance from my higher consciousness and true self. I pray for the wisdom to listen to love instead of fear. I pray for the wisdom, strength and courage to remove myself from noise and stress. I pray for the wisdom to hear and understand my inner voice of intuition. Thank you for blessing me.

Prayer for My Inner Child

Dear Lord,

I pray for the wisdom to have patience with myself. I pray that I am constantly reminded that I am growing and maturing at my own pace. I pray for the wisdom to regularly make time to play and have fun. Thank you for taking care of me.

Prayer to Make Dreams Come True

Dear God,

I pray for the wisdom, strength and courage to hold fast to my faith and expect positive outcomes. I pray for the wisdom, strength and courage to release all fears that could cause me to sabotage my success. I pray for the wisdom to meditate on my desire. I pray for the wisdom, strength and courage to rearrange my schedule so that I am spending time in ways that are truly meaningful to me. Thank you for taking care of me.

Prayer for Spiritual Energy

Dear Masters of the Universe,

I pray for the wisdom to constantly remember how important prayer is. I pray that your will be done every time I pray. I pray for the wisdom to remember that God is the Father and Creator of everything and much more. I pray that my prayers come from love. Thank you for listening to me.

Prayer to Release Personal Ego

Dear Goddess,

I pray for the wisdom to remember that within me lies the center of God's consciousness. I pray for the strength and courage to release my personal ego and to open the door of communication with God. I pray for the wisdom to remember that when I rely on my own beauty, skill or money I am not relying on God. I pray that I remain humble and grateful for all blessings that have been bestowed on me. Thank you for loving me.

Prayer for Love

Dear Higher Power,

I pray to be blessed with unconditional love. I pray for the wisdom to love others unconditionally. Thank you for blessing me.

Prayer to Change my Life

Dear Father,

I pray for the wisdom to be aware that changing my mind will change my life. I pray for the wisdom to remember that if I believe I am unworthy of love and happiness that I will attract to myself situations that disappoint, frustrate and hurt. I pray for the wisdom to remember that my mind is the starting point of every act, thought and feeling. Thank you for loving me.

Prayer for Self-Esteem and Self-Worth

Dear Lord,

I pray that you bless me with an abundance of self-esteem and self-worth. I pray for the wisdom to be able to distinguish self-destructive behavior from productive, healthy behavior. I pray that I never forget my self-worth. I pray for the strength and courage to stand up for my beliefs and myself and not to be bullied into a bad situation just to fit in. I pray for the awareness that my body is a reflection of your creation and it is perfect in every way. Thank you for listening to me.

Prayer for Your Chakras

Dear God,

I pray for the wisdom to balance my chakras. I pray for the wisdom to meditate on my chakras as a powerful way to heal myself. I pray for the wisdom to direct my thoughts to open and balance the spiritual center of my soul. Thank you for loving me.

Prayer for the School of Life

Dear Masters of the Universe,

I pray for the wisdom to remember that the world is not a playground but instead a school. I pray for the wisdom to have fun in my life while being able to learn all of my life lessons. Thank you for taking care of me.

Prayer for Beautiful Thoughts

Dear Goddess,

I pray for the wisdom to remember that every beautiful thought I think about a person, place or thing builds a beautiful soul. Thank you for loving me.

Prayer for Good Judgment

Dear Higher Power,

I pray for the wisdom to make correct choices and to exercise good judgment in every area of my life. Thank you for blessing me.

Prayer to Build Heaven on Earth

Dear Father,

I pray for the wisdom, strength and courage to not judge anything or anyone by only the outer appearances. I pray for the awareness that by judging I am creating a private hell that could permeate the various areas of my life. I pray for the wisdom to realize that if I look outside myself for heaven, I may possibly create a hell of discontent and dissatisfaction for myself. I pray for the wisdom to be reminded that all I really want is not "out there." I pray for the wisdom, strength and courage to remember that I can experience heaven in my own heart. Thank you for loving me.

Prayer for Reputation

Dear Lord,

I pray for the wisdom, strength and courage, as I respond to life's experiences, to make the correct choices that will become the building blocks to create and construct my character. I pray for the wisdom to remember that I am a product of those choices. I pray for the wisdom, strength and courage to be responsible in making the right choice. Thank you for listening to me.

Prayer for Mental Strength and Courage

Dear God,

I pray for mental strength and courage. I pray for the wisdom to make correct choices and to stand up for my beliefs and myself and not to be bullied into a bad situation just to fit in. I pray that you remove any feelings of insecurity that I possess. Thank you for looking out for me.

Prayer to be True to Yourself

Dear Masters of the Universe,

I pray for the courage to stand up for my beliefs and myself and not to be bullied into a bad situation just to fit in. I pray for the wisdom to love my body. Thank you for looking out for me.

Prayer to Learn Life's Purpose

Dear Goddess,

I pray for the wisdom to learn what my life's purpose is. I pray that my intuition will guide me in the right direction. I pray that I will see the correct choices. I pray for the wisdom to remove any anxiety or confusion. I pray for confidence in my abilities. Thank you for taking care of me.

Prayer for Peace and Contentment without Worry, Stress or Anxiety

Dear Higher Power,

I pray that you will bless me with peace and contentment. I pray for the wisdom to remove all worry from my soul. I pray for the strength and courage to recognize contentment without worry. I pray for the wisdom to remove all stress and anxiety. I pray that you remove any feelings of insecurity that I possess. Thank you for listening to me.

Prayer for Happiness

Dear Father,

I pray that you will bless me and those around me with an abundance of happiness. Thank you for blessing me.

Prayer to Live in the Moment

Dear Lord,

I pray for the wisdom to be aware each and every day of my special life. I pray for the wisdom to not take anything for granted and to be grateful for the gift of life. Thank you for blessing me.

Prayer to Forgive Someone

Dear God,

I pray for the wisdom, strength, courage and compassion to forgive the individual who I feel has betrayed me. I pray for the wisdom to see and make the correct choices in this situation. I pray for the courage to stand up for my beliefs and myself and not to be bullied into a bad situation just to fit in. I pray for the wisdom to be able to see the lesson in this situation and to grow from it in a positive way. Thank you for taking care of me.

Prayer for Recognizing my Teacher

Dear Masters of the Universe,

I pray for the wisdom to be able to recognize that everything and everyone in my life are my teachers. I pray for the wisdom to remember that my life is set up to teach me what I need to learn. I pray for the wisdom to be able to recognize that the people I spend most of my time with can tell me much about myself. I pray for the wisdom to remember that what we see in others is a reflection of something within ourselves. I pray for the wisdom to be able to recognize that what we most admire in another may be a quality we possess but have failed to recognize. Thank you for taking care of me.

Prayer for World Peace

Dear Goddess,

I pray for the wisdom to recognize the necessity for a global ethical and spiritual awakening to bring about world peace. I pray that everyone recognizes the importance of individual participation toward this goal. I pray that everyone recognizes that an awakened life is the opportunity to live authentically and in harmony. Thank you for taking care of us.

Prayer to Get the Message

Dear Higher Power,

I pray for the wisdom to learn what I am supposed to learn during my time here on earth. I pray that I will be guided and protected as I walk through life. I pray for the wisdom to see the daily miracles that are so graciously sprinkled in my life. Thank you for taking care of me.

Prayer for Laughter

Dear Father,

I pray for the wisdom to remember that laughter is the best medicine. I pray for the wisdom to be able to laugh at least once a day. I pray for the wisdom to remember that when I laugh many good things will happen. I pray for the wisdom to remember that when I laugh I cannot hold onto negative thoughts. Thank you for loving me.

Prayer for Selflessness

Dear Lord,

I pray for the wisdom to be selfless. I pray that I will be able to help others when needed and not expect anything from them. I am constantly reminded that the payback for selflessness is your blessings in my life. I pray that I am able to care for others from the goodness of my heart. I pray that I have the strength and courage to stand up for my beliefs and myself and not to be bullied into a bad situation just to fit in. Thank you for listening to me.

Prayer to Eliminate Confusion

Dear God,

I am confused and do not know what decision is the correct decision. I pray for a sign that will show me which decision is the correct decision. I pray for the wisdom that I will recognize the sign when presented to me. I pray for the courage to stand up for my beliefs and myself and not to be bullied into a bad situation just to fit in. I pray for the wisdom to be able to see the lesson in this situation and to grow from it in a positive way. Thank you for taking care of me.

Prayer for Humility

Dear Masters of the Universe,

I pray for the wisdom to remember my worth. I thank you for blessing me with special talents and abilities that I can share with the world. I thank you for the creation of my soul and know that mine has an important role in life. I thank you for the unseen beauty that exists as potential inside of me and makes me alive. Thank you for blessing me.

Prayer for the New Year

Dear Goddess,

Thank you for giving me another year here on earth. I am looking forward to new experiences and new lessons. A new chapter in my life is waiting to be written. Thank you for blessing me.

Prayer for Miracles

Dear Higher Power,

Thank you for the many miracles that my life is blessed with every day in every way.

Prayer for Your Angels

Dear Father,

Thank you for my guardian angels that guide me down the necessary paths of life. Thank you for their invisible hands that heal us, touch us and comfort us.

Prayer for the Habit of Being

Dear God,

I pray for the wisdom to experience the habit of being. I pray for the wisdom to live in the present moment. I pray for the wisdom to eliminate the habits of doing and brooding. Thank you for blessing me.

Prayer of Gratitude

Dear Divine One,

I pray for the strength and courage to surrender my desire for security and seek serenity instead. I pray for the wisdom to look at my life with open eyes. I give thanks for all that I have to be grateful for. I pray for forgiveness for the times that I took for granted the riches that already exist in my life. Thank for looking after me.

Prayer to Recognize What You Love

Dear Lord,

I pray for the wisdom to know what I love and not to be influenced by other people or the media. I pray for the wisdom to constantly ask myself what it is that I love. I pray for the strength to have the patience to listen. I pray for the wisdom to know that my life will unfold naturally and with grace. Thank you for listening to me.

Prayer to Simplify Your Life

Dear Masters of the Universe,

I pray for the wisdom and strength to add focus to my life. I pray for the courage and creativity to find the breathing space that I crave. I pray for the strength and courage to eliminate the waste and clutter in my life. Thank you for loving me.

Prayer for Passion

Dear Goddess,

I pray for the wisdom to recognize that every day is an opportunity for me to live my life with passion rather than passive. I pray for the wisdom to remember that passion can transcend and transform my life. Thank you for taking care of me.

Prayer for Simple Pleasures

Dear Higher Power,

I pray for the wisdom to be reminded that my day will be as difficult or as pleasant as I choose to make it. I pray for the wisdom to realize that there is nothing that I can do about my circumstances but accept them. I pray for the wisdom to remind myself, *that it is always my choice.* I pray for the wisdom to be able to enjoy the simple pleasures that I am blessed with in my life. Thank you for loving me.

Prayer for Preserving Time

Dear Divine One,

I pray for the wisdom to make conscious choices. I pray for the wisdom to be aware of how much time I spend in front of the television. I pray for the strength to turn off the television. I pray for the wisdom to reflect on my life and my dreams. Thank you for blessing me.

Prayer to Unlock the Spiritual Mind

Dear Father,

I pray for the wisdom to appeal to the Universe when I feel stuck creatively. I pray for the strength and courage to ask my subconscious to take over when I feel perplexed. I pray for the wisdom to remember that my subconscious mind harnesses an incredible power to assist me with solutions. Thank you for caring about me.

Prayer to Remove the Fear of Death

Dear Lord,

I pray that you will remove any fear that I possess about my life ending. I pray that you will bless me and that I will not suffer. I pray for the wisdom, strength and courage to leave this life. I pray for forgiveness and salvation. I pray that you will heal the pain in the hearts of my friends and families. I pray that they will have the wisdom, strength and courage to continue with their lives in a healthy manner. Thank you for loving me.

Prayer for Your Karma

Dear God,

I pray that you will bless my karma. I pray that you will protect my karma from all evil. I pray for the wisdom to always remember the law of Karma. Thank you for blessing me.

Prayer for Yoga

Dear Goddess,

I pray for the wisdom, strength and courage to perform yoga to the best of my ability. I pray for the wisdom, strength and courage to not judge myself against others. I pray for the wisdom to be able to accept that I am performing at the pace that I am supposed to be. I pray for the wisdom, strength and courage to exercise more mind control and to be able to stop the chatter in my mind. Thank you for blessing me.

Prayer for Transcendental Meditation

Dear Higher Power,

I pray for the wisdom to master this simple, natural effortless technique to gain deep relaxation, eliminate stress, promote my health, and increase my creativity and intelligence to attain an inner happiness and fulfillment. Thank you for taking care of me.

Prayer to Play

Dear Divine One,

I pray for the wisdom to play every day. I pray for the awareness to see the value in playing every day. Thank you for blessing me.

Prayer for the Law of Attraction

Dear Father,

I pray for the wisdom to understand and remember that the Universe responds to what I am thinking. I pray for the wisdom to understand and remember that when I am thinking my situation is bad, the Universe will respond by sending more of what I am thinking. I pray for the wisdom to understand and remember that the Universe does not judge good from bad and only responds by sending more of what I am projecting. I pray for the wisdom and courage to understand my responsibility in the Law of Attraction and what is happening in my life. Thank you for blessing me.

Prayer for Acceptance

Dear God,

I pray for the strength and courage to accept that the only thing that matters is this moment. I pray for the wisdom to know that if I cannot accept where I am right now I will never be able to accept my life as it is. Thank you for blessing them.

Prayer for Seeing a Different Point of View

Dear Goddess,

I pray for the wisdom to be able to see this situation from another point of view. I pray for the wisdom to realize that everything is based on perception. I pray for strength and courage to stand up for my beliefs. Thank you for listening to me.

Prayer to Stay Calm

Dear Higher Power,

I pray for the wisdom, strength and courage to stay calm. I pray for the wisdom to see the benefits of staying calm. Thank you for blessing me.

Prayer to Identify Wastefulness

Dear Father,

I pray for the wisdom to be able to identify wastefulness. I pray for the strength and courage to refrain from being wasteful. I pray for the wisdom to be aware of the ways in which being wasteful is harmful. Thank you for blessing me.

Prayer for Our Planet

Dear Divine One,

I pray that you bless our planet. I pray that everyone be blessed with the wisdom of how valuable our planet is. I pray that everyone be blessed with the strength and courage to treat our planet with the love and respect that it deserves.

Prayer to Wake Up Refreshed

Dear Lord,

I pray for the wisdom to have a good night's sleep which will aid me in waking up refreshed. I pray that upon waking my mind will be clear and sharp. I pray that upon walking my body will be refreshed and full of energy and life. Thank you for blessing me.

Prayer to Stay Focused

Dear God,

I pray for the strength and courage to stay focused. I pray for the wisdom to be aware of how important staying focused is. Thank you for blessing me.

Prayer for a Walk Through

Dear Masters of the Universe,

I pray for the wisdom to understand why a Walk Through has occurred. I pray for the strength and courage to understand that my soul has elevated to a higher level. I pray that you remove any fear that is associated with me letting go of old patterns, behaviors, likes and dislikes. Thank you for listening to me.

Prayer to Define Your Way of Living

Dear Goddess,

I pray for the wisdom to define my way of living. I pray for the strength and courage to stand up for my beliefs and values. I pray for the strength and courage so that I am not encouraged to participate with the masses just to fit in. I pray for the wisdom to have the awareness necessary to define my way of life. Thank you for blessing me.

Prayer for The God I am

Dear Higher Power,

I pray for the wisdom to remember that the God Force is everywhere. I pray for the wisdom to remember that the God Force flows through me and every other living thing on this planet. I pray for the wisdom to remember that I am created in your likeness. I pray for the wisdom to feel the God Force inside of me. Thank you for listening.

Prayer for Understanding What Makes People Tick

Dear Divine One,

I pray for the wisdom to understand what makes people tick. I pray for the strength and courage to let another walk their own path through life. I pray for the wisdom to not take another person's choices personally. I pray for the strength and courage so that I do not control others. I pray for the wisdom to understand that my need to control others comes from my own insecurities. I pray that you remove any insecurity that I may possess. Thank you for taking care of me.

Prayer to Astral Project

Dear Father,

I pray for the wisdom to astral project. I pray for the wisdom to have the proper relaxation and focus in astral projecting. I pray that I am blessed with protection and guidance while I am astral projecting. Thank you for listening to me.

Prayer to Remain Humble

Dear God,

I pray for the wisdom, strength and courage to always remain humble. I pray for the wisdom to be aware of the benefits of remaining humble. Thank you for blessing me.

Prayer to Dream of Past Life Experiences

Dear Lord,

I pray that upon falling asleep I will dream of a past life experience. I pray that I will remember the past life experience upon waking. I pray for the wisdom to learn the lessons necessary from this dream. Thank you for blessing me.

Prayer to Survive Changes in the World

Dear Masters of the Universe,

I pray that I be blessed to survive changes in the world. I pray for the wisdom, strength and courage to be flexible and adapt to the world's changes. I pray that I will be in a position to help others cope with the changes in the world. Thank you for taking care of me.

Prayer to Develop my Psychic Abilities

Dear Higher Power,

I pray for the wisdom to develop my psychic abilities. I pray for the wisdom to be aware of the opportunities in which I can develop my psychic abilities. I pray that I am blessed with protection while developing my psychic abilities. Thank you for blessing me.

Prayer to Visualize Easily & Dimensionally

Dear Goddess,

I pray for the wisdom to visualize easily and dimensionally. I pray for the wisdom, strength and courage to silence the chatter in my mind for better concentration. I pray to be blessed with the ability to focus easily. Thank you for listening to me.

Prayer to Release & Let Go of the Past

Dear Divine One,

I pray for the wisdom, strength and courage to release and let go of the past. I pray for the wisdom to be aware of the benefits of releasing and letting go of the past. I pray for the wisdom to be aware of how not releasing and letting go of the past is harmful to me. Thank you for blessing me.

My Personalized Prayers

My Personalized Prayers

PRAYER FOR/TO

Acceptance.	62
Astral Projection.	73
A Walk Through	69
Be Good to Yourself	8
Be True to Yourself	32
Beautiful Thoughts	27
Break Free.	5
Build Heaven on Earth.	29
Change My Life	23
Define Your Way of Living	70
Detoxification	2
Develop Psychic Abilities	77
Discipline.	16
Dream of Past Life Experience	75
Eliminate Confusion	43
Family Harmony.	14
Feeling Safe	12
Financial Success.	10
Forgive Someone.	37
Get the Message.	40
Good Judgment	28

Gratitude	49
Happiness	35
Higher Consciousness	17
Humility	44
Identify Wastefulness	65
Inner Power	3
Kindness	11
Laughter	41
Learn Life's Purpose	33
Life in the Moment	36
Love	22
Make Dreams Come True	19
Mental Strength and Courage	31
Miracle Healing	4
Miracles	46
My Inner Child	18
Our Planet	66
Passion	52
Peace & Contentment without Worry, Stress or Anxiety	34
Play	60
Preserving Time	54
Recognize What You Love	50

Recognizing my Teacher	38
Release & Let Go of the Past	79
Release Personal Ego	21
Remain Humble	74
Remove Guilt	9
Remove the Fear of Death	56
Reputation	30
Resolution	15
Seeing a Different Point of View	63
Self-Esteem and Self-Worth	24
Self-Reliance	1
Selflessness	42
Simple Pleasures	53
Simplify your Life	51
Spiritual Energy	20
Stay Calm	64
Stay Focused	68
Surrender	7
Survive the World's Changes	76
The God I Am	71
The Habit of Being	48
The Law of Attraction	61
The New Year	45

The School of Life	26
Transcendental Meditation	59
Trust	13
Trust your Intuition	6
Understanding What Makes People Tick	72
Unlock the Spiritual Mind	55
Visualize Easily & Dimensionally	78
Wake up Refreshed	67
World Peace	39
Yoga	58
Your Angels	47
Your Chakras	25
Your Karma	57

www.ingramcontent.com/pod-product-compliance
Lightning Source LLC
Chambersburg PA
CBHW032018040426
42448CB00006B/657